UNDERSTANDING
POLITICAL
SYSTEMS

WHAT IS COMMUNISM?

KAREN LATCHANA KENNEY

raintree
a Capstone company — publishers for children

Raintree is an imprint of Capstone Global Library Limited, a company incorporated in England and Wales having its registered office at 264 Banbury Road, Oxford OX2 7DY – Registered company number: 6695582

www.raintree.co.uk
myorders@raintree.co.uk

Produced for Raintree by Calcium
Edited by Sarah Eason and John Andrews
Designed by Keith Williams
Picture research by Rachel Blount
Production by Victoria Fitzgerald
Originated by Capstone Global Library Ltd © 2017
Printed and bound in Hong Kong

ISBN 978 1 4747 3117 1
20 19 18 17 16
10 9 8 7 6 5 4 3 2 1

British Library Cataloguing in Publication Data
A full catalogue record for this book is available from the British Library

Acknowledgements
We would like to thank the following for permission to reproduce photographs: Dreamstime: Abc745172003 23, Baz777 39, Rafael Ben-ari 1, 37, Dmitry424 7, Erikdegraaf 21, Harryfn 36, Id1974 17, Itpow 28, Ivanmakarov 15, Izf 32, Jochenschneider 31, Kspr84 41, Wendy Leber 27, Linqong 19, 24, 43, 45, Roman Milert 20, Roland Nagy 26, Patje888 30, Wanghanan 14, Witoldkr1 38, Yuri4u80 10; Shutterstock: Hung Chung Chih 4, 44, Fourb 35, IgorGolovniov 33, Kobby Dagan 18, Lane Ergle 8, Oleg Golovnev 9, Muellek Josef 42, Jps 11, John Lock 13, Marzolino 16, Neftali 5, Neveshkin Nikolay 6, Krzysztof Stepien 12, Testing 22, 29, 40, Ahmad Faizal Yahya 34, Claudio Zaccherini 25.

Cover art reproduced with permission of: Shutterstock: Iryna1 (left), Volkova Natalia (right).

Every effort has been made to contact copyright holders of material reproduced in this book. Any omissions will be rectified in subsequent printings if notice is given to the publisher.

All the internet addresses (URLs) given in this book were valid at the time of going to press. However, due to the dynamic nature of the internet, some addresses may have changed, or sites may have changed or ceased to exist since publication. While the author and publisher regret any inconvenience this may cause readers, no responsibility for any such changes can be accepted by either the author or the publisher.

Contents

CHAPTER ONE

What is communism?

The communist system began as an ideal – it was a way to share the wealth created in a country and eliminate social classes. This system arose in the mid-1800s and was adopted by many countries in the 1900s. Although few countries are communist today, it is the system of government in the country with the most people in the world – China. **Communism** is distinctly different from other forms of government and can be considered the opposite of capitalism.

A CLASSLESS SOCIETY

The communist ideal is to create a society without social classes and to equally share the wealth of a country. A social class is a group of people who share the same economic status. In a society with classes, people can be grouped into upper, middle, working and poor classes. The upper classes are wealthy and may control businesses and land, and have power and influence. Lower classes have less money and influence, and they struggle more to obtain the basic necessities of life.

Chinese soldiers patrol an area of Beijing, China, in 2012.

CUBA
correos

50 ANIVERSARIO DEL MINREX

2009

▲ *Fidel Castro was the communist leader of Cuba for decades.*

In a communist society, the government controls the economy, and there is only one political party. There is no private ownership of land or capital. In theory, everything becomes public and is shared for the benefit of the group, rather than the benefit of the individual.

THE SINGLE-PARTY SYSTEM

In many countries, there are several political parties, each representing different values and views for the country. Voters then choose the party candidates they favour in an election. In a communist system, voters are offered just one party: the communist party. Elections may be held, but the candidates will only belong to the communist party.

UNDERSTANDING BETTER

WHAT IS A DICTATORSHIP?

Communist leaders have often become **dictators**. A dictator is a person who has absolute power over a country and is not limited by laws or a **constitution**. Dictators often rule a country for decades. Here are some of the world's longest-ruling communist dictators:

- Fidel Castro: leader of Cuba for 49 years

- Kim Il-sung: leader of North Korea for 46 years

- Mao Zedong: leader of China for 31 years

- Joseph Stalin: leader of the USSR for 29 years

- Ho Chi Minh: leader of North Vietnam for 24 years

What does their length of rule tell you about communist dictators? How do you think these dicators stayed in power for so many years?

The history of communism

The idea of a society where goods are shared equally has been around since the fourth century BC. The ancient Greek **philosopher** Plato wrote about it in his book *The Republic*. He believed that when individuals owned goods, it made them selfish. Plato thought that there should be a group of guardians who made sure that all goods were shared among the community.

A NEW CLASS OF WORKERS

In the Industrial Revolution of the 1800s, a large working class arose. This was a time when new machinery, fuels, building materials and work systems were developed, which made it possible to create large quantities of goods quickly and cheaply in factories. People moved to growing cities to work in those factories, becoming the working class. The owners of big businesses grew wealthy, but the working class did not make much money, worked long hours with few breaks and lived in poor conditions.

Workers made goods quickly and cheaply in factories during the Industrial Revolution, such as this textile factory in England.

THE MEN BEHIND COMMUNISM

German philosopher Karl Marx noticed these class differences and believed European society was corrupt. He thought it could not be fixed and had to change. He joined with his friend Friedrich Engels, another German philosopher, to write a pamphlet that was critical of **capitalism** and that outlined a new type of society – a communist society. This pamphlet, *Manifesto of the Communist Party*, was published in 1848. It called upon the workers of the world to unite and fight against the capitalist system and the classes in charge. Marx's theory, called **Marxism**, also explained how **revolutions** could be used to overthrow capitalism and replace it with communism.

Statues of Karl Marx and Friedrich Engels, the famous communist philosophers, stand in Berlin, Germany.

UNDERSTANDING BETTER

KARL MARX AND HIS THEORIES

The following quote is from the final section of the *Manifesto of the Communist Party*.

"In short, the communists everywhere support every revolutionary movement against the existing social and political order of things. The communists … openly declare that their ends can be attained only by the forcible overthrow of all existing social conditions. Let the ruling classes tremble at a communistic revolution."

What does the quote tell you about Karl Marx and Friedrich Engels? What kind of emotion does their writing instil in the reader? Is it passionate, threatening or bland? How do you think others took the message of Marx and Engels at the time?

Lenin and the Bolshevik revolution

Marx died in 1883, but Engels continued with his work. After the death of Engels in 1895, Marxist followers split into two groups. One group believed that the transition to communism should be peaceful and happen gradually, the other believed revolution was necessary to make the change.

LENIN AND COMMUNISM

Vladimir Lenin was a political leader in Russia in the early 1900s. His party, the Russian Social-Democratic Workers' Party, believed that the best way to achieve communism was through revolution. Most people in Russia at the time were poor **peasant** farmers who worked land owned by wealthy nobles, and they were unhappy with the system of government. Lenin believed that the country was ready for a revolution, led by a ruling party made up of knowledgeable people, or **intellectuals**, like himself, who would decide on a direction for the good of the people. The people would not be able to debate or change that direction, which meant that the party would have to enforce strict rules that everyone would have to follow.

Vladimir Lenin was the leader of the communist party in Russia in the early 1900s.

Tsar Nicholas II and the rest of the Romanov family were the last royal family to rule in Russia.

THE RUSSIAN REVOLUTION

In 1917, the leader of Russia was **Tsar** Nicholas II, a monarch whose father had been the previous leader. The people were not happy because Russia had lost many soldiers during World War I (1914–1918) and because of food shortages in the country. Riots broke out, the tsar was forced to step down and the Russian parliament appointed a temporary government. However, another party soon took over – the communists, led by Lenin, who called themselves the **Bolsheviks**, meaning "the majority". This new government seized control of the country's industries and land owned by the nobles, then gave that land to the peasants. Russia had become the first communist country, and its empire was formed into the Union of Soviet **Socialist** Republics (USSR).

UNDERSTANDING BETTER

THE OLD RULERS OF RUSSIA

For centuries, tsars had total power over Russia. They did not necessarily know how to run a country but made decisions that affected all of Russia's people. The tsars and their families had lavish lifestyles, wore furs and jewels and lived in extravagant palaces. After reading about the tsars, can you understand better why the peasants were unhappy with their country's leadership? What do you think they thought about the tsars and the luxurious way they lived?

Stalin and the Iron Curtain

Lenin ruled Russia until his death in 1924. This left three other Bolshevik leaders – Joseph Stalin, Leon Trotsky and Nikolai Bukharin – in power. Stalin wanted to be the sole leader of the USSR, so he had Trotsky and Bukharin removed from power. He then sent millions of people he claimed to be spies or against the party to prison, or to labour camps in a remote and desolate region called Siberia, and had thousands of people executed. Stalin gained control and introduced his own form of communism – Stalinism.

Joseph Stalin claimed power over the USSR after Lenin's death.

WHAT DID STALIN BELIEVE?

Under Stalin, communism was changed to fit his needs. He thought a communist leader should be able to do whatever he thought was best, even if it went against communist ideals. Stalin also said that the communist party was filled with traitors and that the power needed to rest on one supreme leader – himself. Stalin developed a **cult of personality**, using media, control and **propaganda** to build a presence about himself as an absolute ruler, almost like a king.

British prime minister Winston Churchill fought against the spread of communism.

UNDERSTANDING BETTER

THE IRON CURTAIN

Winston Churchill was the prime minister of the United Kingdom from 1940 to 1945. In one of his famous speeches, he coined the term "Iron Curtain". Here is an excerpt from that speech, made in 1946:

"From Stettin in the Baltic to Trieste in the Adriatic, an iron curtain has descended across the Continent. … The communist parties, which were very small in all these eastern states of Europe, have been raised to pre-eminence and power far beyond their numbers and are seeking everywhere to obtain [total] control."

What does this quote tell you about the term "Iron Curtain"? What do you think it means, and why do you think that Churchill chose those words?

COMMUNISM SPREADS ACROSS EUROPE

After World War II, Stalin set up communist systems in other eastern European countries, including Czechoslovakia, Poland, Hungary, Yugoslavia, Romania, Albania and East Germany. These communist countries created a geographical divider between the USSR and central and western Europe. This barrier, called the **Iron Curtain**, separated communist and non-communist countries. Behind the Iron Curtain, the USSR became totally isolated from the international community.

Communism in China

While communism was growing in the USSR, it was also developing in China. The Chinese Communist Party took control of the government in 1949. Its leader was Mao Zedong, who developed his own form of communism, called Maoism.

WHAT IS MAOISM?

Unlike communism in the USSR, Maoism focused more on the rural peasants than the urban workers. At the time in China, there were hundreds of millions of peasants living in poverty, and Mao believed that they were the revolutionary force that could overthrow the government. This peasant force was the basis for Mao's communist rule.

His belief in the power of this force led to a plan, called the Great Leap Forward, to speed up China's industry. The plan, which lasted from 1958 to 1960, encouraged peasants to form communities, called **collectives**, to produce steel in home-made furnaces. This effort turned into a national disaster, disrupting agriculture and causing less food to be produced. As a result, around 20 million Chinese people starved to death between 1959 and 1962.

▼ *A statue of Mao Zedong stands in Kashgar, China.*

UNDERSTANDING BETTER

MAO'S PROPAGANDA

Mao Zedong used propaganda to spread his messages of communism during the Cultural Revolution. Look at this poster from that time. Mao is the head in the sky, and the people below are holding his book of communist ideals, known in Western countries as the "Little Red Book". What does this piece of propaganda tell you about his rule of communist China? How is Mao portrayed in this image?

A Chinese propaganda poster from the 1970s shows a message of the Cultural Revolution.

CHANGING THE NATIONAL CULTURE

In 1966, Mao launched a new campaign, called the Cultural Revolution. He wanted to promote the values of peasant life, while removing the influence of intellectuals and the **elite**, and so urged the youth of China to rid their country of foreign cultural elements. As a result, children reported their parents to the police if they believed them to be against Mao, people who were thought to be traitors were killed or imprisoned, urban teenagers were ordered to move to rural areas to work on farms, and literature and music from Western countries were banned. A new culture was installed, which included Chinese revolutionary songs and poems, and new art and opera. This created a cult of personality around Mao, who led the country until his death in 1976. China is still under communist rule today.

Modern communism

Communism reached its peak in the 1900s. At one time, nearly one-third of the world's people lived in countries with communist systems. The USSR collapsed in 1991, bringing an end to communism there, and today only five countries are still under communist rule – China, Cuba, Vietnam, Laos and North Korea. All of these countries, except for North Korea, have made moves towards capitalism, allowing at least some economic competition.

NORTH KOREA

The communist party came to power in North Korea in 1946, and its first leader was Kim Il-sung. When he died, in 1991, his son, Kim Jong-il, took control.

When Kim Jong-il died in 2011, his son, Kim Jong-un, became the leader. The Kim family has kept tight control over North Korea for more than 60 years. It is the only country in the world that still follows the strict USSR style of communism.

A statue of Kim Il-sung stands in front of a North Korean building.

A statue of US soldiers stands in memory of the many lives lost during the Vietnam War.

CUBA, VIETNAM AND LAOS

The small Latin American island of Cuba became communist in 1959, when a revolutionary leader called Fidel Castro led a rebel army that overthrew the government. Castro remained president of the country until 2008, when his brother, Raul Castro, took over.

In 1954, the Southeast Asian country of Vietnam split into North Vietnam and South Vietnam. The north became communist, while the south was anti-communist. The United States fought to keep communism out of the south but did not succeed, and, in 1975, North Vietnam took control of the south, uniting the country under communist rule.

Next to Vietnam is the country of Laos. It became communist in 1975, establishing a similar type of rule as that in Vietnam. Laos's communist government replaced a monarchy that had ruled the country for 600 years.

UNDERSTANDING BETTER

THE VIETNAM WAR

From 1965 to 1973, the United States fought in Vietnam to try to stop the spread of communism, which it feared would spread to other Asian countries. The war had deadly effects, with around 200,000–250,000 South Vietnamese soldiers and 58,000 US soldiers killed. The fighting took place mostly in the thick jungle of Vietnam, where the communist soldiers knew how to move and hide better than the US soldiers. In the end, the United States withdrew and Vietnam became a communist country. Why do you think the United States became involved in the communist struggle in Vietnam?

CHAPTER TWO

The communist system

In their *Manifesto*, Marx and Engels outlined a plan to set up a communist government in a country. This became the basis for communist movements around the world.

THE BOURGEOISIE AND THE PROLETARIAT

Marx and Engels believed that there were two main classes of people in modern capitalist society – the **bourgeoisie** and the **proletariat**. The bourgeoisie were the upper class. They had political power, made political decisions that benefited their class, and controlled much of the land and the production of goods.

The proletariat were the modern working class of people, who laboured in factories, basically helping machines do the work needed to produce goods. They were paid just enough to live but not enough to have a decent life. However, Marx and Engels believed in the strength of this class, once its people were united, and thought that they were the people who could cause change in the political system. The communist party aligned with the working class people, choosing to represent the needs of the proletariat.

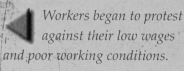

Workers began to protest against their low wages and poor working conditions.

TIME FOR REVOLUTION

According to Marx and Engels, capitalist society could not be fixed. It had to be overthrown and replaced with a communist structure, which would ideally focus on the needs of the masses, rather than those of the ruling few. However, for that new structure to take hold, revolution had to take place. This meant that the proletariat would have to join together and take control of the government by force. Once in power, the proletariat would then install a communist regime.

Karl Marx wrote about the basic principles of communism in Manifesto of the Communist Party.

UNDERSTANDING BETTER

THE 10 BASIC MEASURES OF COMMUNISM

In their *Manifesto*, Marx and Engels outlined 10 basic measures that would have to take place after a revolution. They included the ideas that all land should be publicly owned, the government should control all banks and most factories, and that education should be free for all children in public schools. Do you think that these are major or minor changes? Do you think it was easy or difficult for people to give up their land to the government after it became communist?

Command economy

Different communist countries operate in different ways, but they all have a kind of economic system, called a **command economy**, which is very different from the market economy in the United Kingdom. In a market economy, the production of goods is based on what consumers need. The consumers buy what they need at certain prices, which then lets the suppliers know what goods are required and how quickly and at what price they should sell the goods. In a command economy, the government tells suppliers what and how many goods they need to make and what prices suppliers can charge for those goods.

THE GOVERNMENT IN CONTROL

In a communist country, the government controls the production of all goods and sets production goals for industries. The government also controls the amount of raw materials each supplier can have in order to produce the amount of goods needed to reach their goals.

The government controls the goods made in China.

18

North Korean shops sell limited amounts of goods.

UNDERSTANDING BETTER

NORTH KOREAN SHORTAGES

According to a 22 April 2013 *Wall Street Journal* article, North Korea asked Mongolia, a country bordering Russia and China, for food aid because of its shortages. The article states:

"Ambassador Hong Gyu told President Elbegdorj 'North Korea may face [a] severe food shortage'. Mr Hong then asked for Mongolia to consider the possibility of delivering food aid to North Korea.

North Korea's toughest part of the year for food begins in April and runs through September, when the annual corn harvest begins."

Compare this information with the main text. What does the article tell you that the text does not?

EFFICIENT OR DANGEROUS?

In theory, the practice of controlling production leads to a more efficient use of natural resources. It should also help the government provide, when needed, a large amount of goods in a short time, which is especially helpful after a natural disaster. However, consumers have limited choices of goods, and the country may also experience shortages of certain goods if demands are higher than the country's set production goals.

The USSR's command economy caused major shortages of food and goods. North Korea still follows the Soviet-style command economy, and its people have experienced many food shortages as a result. China, Cuba and Vietnam have all made changes towards market economies.

Media control and propaganda

The media, which includes newspapers, television and the internet, is a powerful tool. It can be used to spread information and persuade the public about different ideas. Communist countries control the media and stop information that they believe to be against the government. Many communist governments also spread the party's message to the people of the country by saying positive things about themselves and negative things about their enemies, even if they are lies. This is called "propaganda".

CENSORING THE MEDIA

The press, such as newspapers and magazines, is tightly controlled in communist countries, and certain stories may be edited or even banned by people, called censors, who check all areas of the media. According to the Worldwide Press Freedom Index of 2016, communist countries rank low in terms of press freedom. Of the 180 countries in the list, North Korea was at 179, China 176, Vietnam 175, Laos 173 and Cuba 171. In comparison, the press in Finland, Netherlands and Norway – all democratic countries – had the most freedom.

Communist governments often censor what is shown on the internet in their countries.

Journalists in communist countries have often been arrested and put in prison for writing stories that were critical of the government, or that included information the government did not want released. For example, Reporters Without Borders, an organization that was set up to protect journalists, reported that 49 journalists were in Chinese prisons in 2015.

THE POWER OF PROPAGANDA

A poster, a statue, a song or even a poem can be a piece of propaganda. What all propaganda contains is a message that promotes a certain political view. Sometimes, these messages come in the form of a slogan. Many times, propaganda spreads false information. All communist countries use some form of political propaganda to try to convince people and control opinion.

UNDERSTANDING BETTER

LENIN'S SLOGAN

Lenin, the first leader of the USSR, used the following slogan as propaganda:

"The dictatorship of the proletariat will bring us from capitalism's gloom and oppression to a radiant future [under communism]."

What do you think the above slogan means? Do you think the information it contains is true or false?

A Vietnamese poster shows a communist message.

Government structure

In a communist country, the communist party controls all aspects of the government. The leader of the communist party is also the chief executive of the country's government. Typically, there is no term limit for this leader. This person can serve for a lifetime, as many communist leaders, such as Mao Zedong and Kim Jong-il, have. While each communist government has its differences, most have a similar structure. Here is how China's communist government is structured.

POLITBURO AND LEGISLATURE

Although the leader has the final decision, issues are first discussed within a group of advisers. In China, this group is called the **politburo**. It has 25 members, all of whom are men. The members of the politburo debate an issue and then make their decision about how to act. This decision then becomes a policy, and the politburo members are bound to that policy.

These are China's government buildings. The policies of the politburo are carried out by government ministers and workers.

MAKING LAW

The **legislature**, or law-making body, in China is the National People's Congress. It is a parliament with nearly 3,000 members. This large group does not do much of the work, however. It is done, instead, by a select committee of about 150 members. In theory, the legislature has the power to change the constitution and make laws. In reality, it gives its official stamp to the policies decided by the leader and the politburo. Smaller local legislatures deal with local issues.

STATE COUNCIL

The task of the State Council is to make sure that the government carries out the communist party's decisions. This department drafts the country's economic plans and budgets, setting five-year plans for the country's economic course. In 2016, China released its 13th five-year plan.

UNDERSTANDING BETTER

ELECTIONS IN CHINA

In China, elections are held for legislative representatives at local levels. However, most people do not take the legislature seriously, believing it has no real power. Candidates only belong to the communist party and are approved by the party. Voters do not have much of a choice but are required to vote. After reading about Chinese elections, compare what you have learned with what you know about United Kingdom elections. How are Chinese elections similar or different?

In Chinese elections, all candidates belong to the communist party.

Cult of personality

For many communist leaders, having a cult of personality helps to control the public. A cult of personality is an idealized public image that is developed through the use of media, propaganda and, sometimes, false information. The leader who has this image becomes almost god-like to the public, and can then say or do things with little public doubt or questioning. It is an especially helpful position for a dictator to hold. Several communist leaders have been known for their larger-than-life cult of personality.

MAO ZEDONG

During the Cultural Revolution, Mao Zedong's personality cult grew. His image and slogans could be seen everywhere, from the badges that people wore and his "Little Red Book" of sayings to large murals in public spaces. Images showed Mao holding babies or standing in front of large amounts of food and included sayings such as "Turn China into a prosperous, rich and powerful industrialized **socialist** country under the leadership of the Communist Party and Chairman Mao!" Even children's toys and books contained messages about Mao and communism.

A large portrait shows a smiling Kim Il-sung in Pyongyang, North Korea.

위대한수령김일성동지는영원히우리와함께계신다

Mao Zedong's "Little Red Book" contains quotes from the leader.

UNDERSTANDING BETTER

MAO'S "LITTLE RED BOOK"

Members of the Red Guard, which was the youth group during the Cultural Revolution, always carried a book of quotations by their leader, Mao, which became known in the West as the "Little Red Book". Here is an excerpt:

"Our duty is to hold ourselves responsible to the people. Every word, every act and every policy must conform to the people's interests, and, if mistakes occur, they must be corrected – that is what being responsible to the people means."

Think about how this helped Mao's cult of personality. Why do you think this quote was included in the "Little Red Book"? Do you think the government and the Red Guard followed this advice?

NORTH KOREAN LEADERS

The communist government of North Korea strictly controls its people. That is why a cult of personality is so important to its leaders. The country's one television channel has programmes showing the leader Kim Jong-un as a kind of rock star, who is chased by his fans, and huge portraits of the late leaders Kim Il-sung and Kim Jong-Il tower over public squares. Having such a strong cult of personality has helped the Kim family stay in power for decades.

T047349

CHAPTER THREE

Living with communism

In a democratic society, people enjoy many freedoms. They have free speech, a free press and the right to protest. They can freely use the internet and read news from other countries. However, life in a communist country is very different, with many freedoms restricted and information controlled. These controls are part of daily life in a communist country.

INTERNET AND SOCIAL MEDIA

It was easier to control information before the evolution of the internet, which allowed information to be quickly spread around the world. What worries communist governments is that their country's people may read or spread information that criticizes or undermines the government. To combat this spread of information, China has developed an internet-filtering system that controls who has access to the internet and what content can be accessed. For example, searching for "Democracy movements" will lead to a blank screen that states, "Page cannot be displayed". North Korea completely bans the general public from going online.

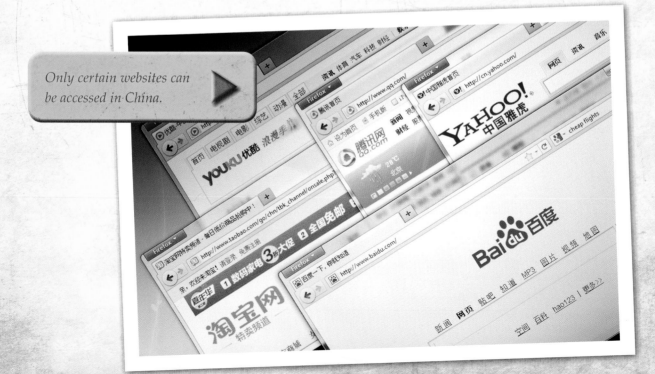

Only certain websites can be accessed in China.

Blogging is also restricted in communist countries. Some bloggers find unusual ways to post their blogs, though. In Cuba, internet access for the general public is limited, and most people can only open an email account that can be used at post offices. One Cuban blogger, Yoani Sánchez, sneaks into tourist hotels to use the guests' computers. She has to type quickly to make sure she will not be caught. In China, the government simply shuts down blogs if it believes the posted messages are at all inappropriate.

A group of sculptures by Chinese artist Ai Weiwei, including a chicken's head, went on an international tour in 2011.

UNDERSTANDING BETTER

ONE ARTIST AGAINST THE SYSTEM

Modern artist Ai Weiwei uses social media and art to protest against the Chinese political system and stand up for **human rights** in his country. On Twitter, he voices his thoughts about **censorship** and freedom, and his art makes statements about issues in China. Through Twitter, Weiwei escapes the censorship enforced by the government on other forms of media. Weiwei has said of Twitter:

"Twitter is my city, my favourite city. I can talk to anybody I want to. And anybody who wants to talk to me will get my response. They know me better than their relatives or my relatives."

After reading about Weiwei, what do you think this quote means? What is the importance of Twitter to Weiwei and the Chinese people?

Prison camps and corruption

Speaking out in a communist country is a risk. Many journalists have been sent to prison for reporting news the government did not want to be released, and police have detained bloggers and activists without being charged. Sometimes people are sent to harsh prison camps. The police rarely help people. Many are corrupt, and they accept bribes and use violence to get people to do as they wish.

THE PRISON CAMP THREAT

North Korea has a large network of prison camps, with perhaps as many as 200,000 people imprisoned in them. Little is known about the camps, except through the few accounts from people who have escaped. The North Korean government denies that the camps even exist.

One escapee, Shin Dong-hyuk, was born inside a camp and lived there for 23 years before escaping. He told the American television news programme *60 Minutes* how prisoners are treated inside the camp. They are beaten and tortured, and many starve to death. After Shin accidentally broke a machine in a factory, the tip of his finger was cut off as a punishment.

In China, many thousands of people are sent to prison camps for crimes such as stealing, using drugs or prostitution. They can be forced to work in prison camps for up to four years, without being tried or charged in a court.

People can be sent to prison camps in communist countries.

CORRUPTION CHINESE-STYLE

In China, many government officials and police officers are corrupt. They may accept bribes to make sure certain building projects are approved, or use violence to make people do what they want. Few are ever punished for corrupt behaviour. Without any opposition, the communist party can get away with its actions. However, a growing number of Chinese citizens are using the internet to expose this **corruption**.

UNDERSTANDING BETTER

CORRUPT OFFICIALS AND FAST CARS

In Beijing, the capital of China, some police and government officials drive Porsches and Bentleys worth as much as £400,000. The government pays for these expensive cars but finds it hard to fund school buses. It makes the Chinese public angry. One activist wrote:

"You can't get evidence about other kinds of corruption, such as people accepting envelopes of cash, but this you easily see for yourself."

What does this tell you about the system in China? How would you feel if you knew the police and government officials in your country were driving such expensive, state-bought cars?

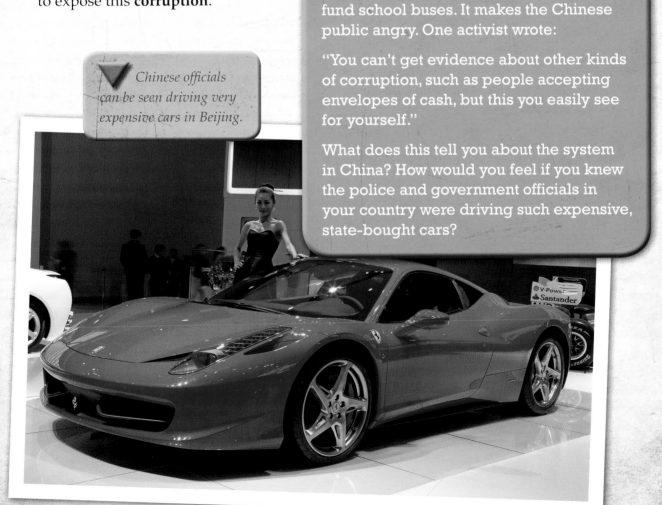

Chinese officials can be seen driving very expensive cars in Beijing.

Shortages and the black market

Because of the command economies in communist countries, shortages are common. If the production of goods does not meet the need for those goods, shortages occur and people may wait for hours in long queues to get a loaf of bread or piece of meat. The government rations the supplies to make them last longer, but the people may then lack enough food to feed their families.

NOT ENOUGH TO GO AROUND

Many North Korean children suffer from malnutrition because of food shortages. According to a United Nations (UN) statement in 2016, 18 million North Koreans were in need of food assistance. Fuel and equipment shortages affect food production in the country as well.

Without tractors that work, farmers are unable to plant and harvest crops to feed the country's 24 million people.

In Cuba, food shortages make the price of food rise higher, and that causes the prices of other goods to also rise. Sometimes, there is enough food, but it goes to waste because of poor management of the food supply. In January 2013, 90 tonnes (89 tons) of tomatoes spoiled in a badly run government storage area in Cuba. No one had arranged for the tomatoes to be shipped to the markets, and the produce went bad.

A shop in Havana, Cuba, has few items on its shelves.

If they can afford to, North Koreans buy food and other goods from the black market.

SHOPPING ON THE BLACK MARKET

People in communist countries must sometimes buy goods from the black market to meet their needs. A black market is an illegal system of trade, where goods may be sold at very high prices. In communist countries with shortages, those with the money can supplement their basic food supply with goods from the black market.

UNDERSTANDING BETTER

A CRAVING FOR CHOCO PIES

One favourite item sold on the black market in North Korea is the Choco Pie, a chocolate-covered snack made of two cakes filled with marshmallow. North Koreans cannot buy these snacks in the government markets, but they are in great demand, so traders go to China or South Korea to buy them and then make large profits selling them in the North Korean black market. What does this tell you about the North Korean people? Do you think they are isolated in their country? Do you think they have all that they want or need?

Healthcare

In communist countries, medical services are either free or mostly covered by the government. However, the quality of these services varies from country to country.

CHINA

In China, the healthcare system is much better now than it was in the 1980s and 1990s. The system was reformed after 2009, and now around 95 per cent of the population is covered by public health insurance, although this only pays for half of most hospital costs. Some hospitals have to limit the stays of very ill people to two weeks because the government will only pay the hospitals so much per year, and longer stays use too much of that money. Other hospitals simply refuse to admit ill patients.

NORTH KOREA

Amnesty International, a human rights organization, reported in 2010 that North Korea's healthcare system is in a terrible state. Interviews with 40 former North Koreans tell of the poor medical care in the country, including the amputation of one man's leg without the use of any anaesthetic. Although healthcare is supposed to be free, the government seems to pay its doctors poorly and provides limited supplies. Patients must bring money or goods to give to doctors or they may not be treated.

Patients wait to be treated at a Chinese hospital.

Día Mundial de la Salud

Cuba
Correos
1973

25
ANIVERSARIO

A 1973 Cuban stamp emphasizes the importance of infant healthcare.

CUBA

The healthcare system in Cuba is very good in comparison to China. All care is absolutely free and the system is focused on preventing major health problems. People live to an average age of 78 years old, and health education is taught in schools. Every patient gets a yearly doctor's visit at home. However, there is little patient choice and the doctors' resources are limited.

UNDERSTANDING BETTER

CUBAN AND UK HEALTHCARE

Cuba can match some of the health statistics found in the United Kingdom. Life expectancy in Cuba is only slightly less, and its infant death numbers are the same as those of the United Kingdom. Doctors work for the government and are paid low salaries, but they receive free education and a home. What do you think about the system in Cuba? Do you think it is as good as, better or worse than the system in the United Kingdom?

Education and youth

Free education for all children was one of the founding principles of communism, as described by Marx and Engels in their *Manifesto*. Education is a very important issue in communist countries. Some countries have good educational systems and high literacy rates, but there are still costs to students' parents, and the government sets the curriculum. The government can then use education as a way to spread its political messages.

CHINA AND VIETNAM

The Chinese government provides schooling from primary school all the way up through four years of university education. According to United Nations (UN) statistics, China's literacy rate in 2015 was 99.7 per cent. In 2013, students in Shanghai, a large city in China, showed the highest scores in the world in maths, science and reading. However, that high level of education is not the same throughout the country. There are big differences between rural and urban schools, with some rural families paying up to half of their small incomes for school transport or boarding costs.

Vietnam has a high literacy rate and a large national university. According to UN statistics, 98 per cent of Vietnam's citizens above the age of 15 can read and write. However, some say the system is old-fashioned and that it is also flawed due to heavy censorship.

School is free for children aged between 6 and 11 in Vietnam.

LIFE IN CUBA

There is a high literacy rate in Cuba. Around 99.9 per cent of its population can read and write, which is as high as the rate in the United Kingdom. Education is free, but the government sets the places available for study each year in the universities. This is related to which industries the government wants to promote. For example, in 2012 more farmers and skilled workers were needed, so the numbers of places leading to professional careers were lowered to reflect that.

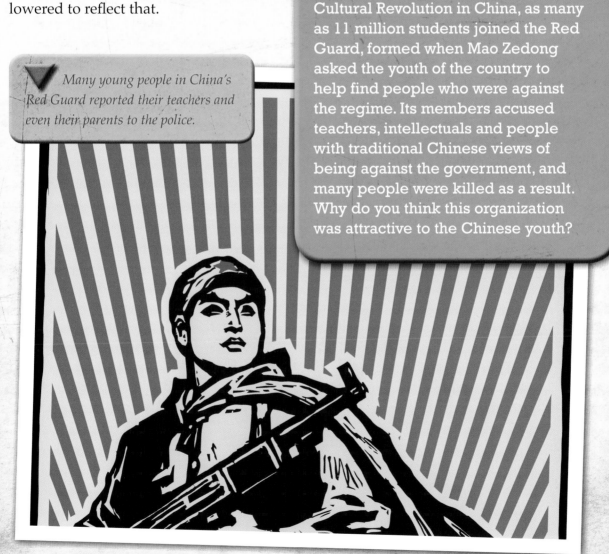

Many young people in China's Red Guard reported their teachers and even their parents to the police.

UNDERSTANDING BETTER

MOBILIZING THE YOUTH OF THE COUNTRY

Youth organizations can be used to spread political messages. During the Cultural Revolution in China, as many as 11 million students joined the Red Guard, formed when Mao Zedong asked the youth of the country to help find people who were against the regime. Its members accused teachers, intellectuals and people with traditional Chinese views of being against the government, and many people were killed as a result. Why do you think this organization was attractive to the Chinese youth?

CHAPTER FOUR

Fighting against communism

Although communism was gaining strength in the mid-1900s, many democratic countries around the world fought against its spread. People living in communist countries also staged demonstrations against their controlling governments.

INTERNATIONAL OPPOSITION

In the 1940s and 1950s, extreme tension grew between the United States and the USSR, which was known as the **Cold War**. The United States joined with the United Kingdom and other countries in Europe to form the North Atlantic Treaty Organization (NATO), which was a unified military force against the Soviets. The Cold War continued until the collapse of the USSR in 1991.

During the 1960s, Cuba and the USSR posed a nuclear threat to the United States and other Western countries. During the Cuban Missile Crisis in 1962, there was almost a nuclear war between the two sides. As a result, the United States blocked all trade with Cuba and travel to the country was banned. Since 2000, some trade and travel bans have been lifted, and in 2015 the United States and Cuba renewed diplomatic relations.

USSR missiles were ready to launch against Western targets during the Cold War.

Chinese soldiers march in Tiananmen Square.

MAKING PROTESTS

People living in communist countries have protested, but the governments usually quickly stop them, and protesters can be put in prison and even executed. One of the most well known Chinese activists is Liu Xiaobo. He participated in a protest in Tiananmen Square, Beijing, in 1989, and wrote a manifesto, called *Charter 08*, which called for political change in China. Liu was arrested in 2009 for writing the charter and was sentenced to 11 years in prison. In 2010, he was awarded the Nobel Peace Prize for his human rights work.

UNDERSTANDING BETTER

TIANANMEN SQUARE PROTEST

In the late 1980s, there was a growing anti-communist movement in China, especially among university students. On 22 April 1989, students gathered in Tiananmen Square, a large square in Beijing, to protest for their rights. By mid-May, there were nearly 1 million people demonstrating, so in June the government responded, sending tanks and armed troops into the square, shooting at the protestors and killing or wounding many. Thousands were imprisoned. Why do you think the government reacted in this way? Do you think it was right or wrong? What do you think people around the world felt or thought after seeing the government's reaction on television?

North Korean threats

North Korea is a highly secretive country. It lets little information in to the country – and even less out. However, the messages North Korea does send out are often threats aimed at the United States and South Korea. North Korean propaganda claims the country has far more strength than most people believe it actually does.

NUCLEAR WEAPONS AND MISSILES

The two superpowers – the United States and the USSR – stopped testing nuclear weapons in the 1990s. Testing a nuclear weapon is a way to show the world what kind of military strength a country has. North Korea has tested nuclear weapons four times – in 2006, 2009, 2013 and 2016 – and it has also launched missiles. Some missile tests were failures, but others have succeeded. The country issues daily threats to the United States and South Korea, stating that it will attack if provoked. The United States does not believe North Korea has the ability to attack. However, the United States also knows North Korea is working on developing its nuclear weapons.

North Korea has tested nuclear weapons since 2006.

INTERNATIONAL RESPONSE

Several countries have reacted to the nuclear tests, missile launchings and threats. The United States has stopped food aid to North Korea and has imposed laws, called **sanctions**, to stop people doing business with the country. China has made sanctions against North Korean banking, travel and trade, and Japan has cut off its funding for a North Korean energy project. The United Nations (UN) has also imposed penalties on the country, banning its nuclear-testing programme. The UN also bans trade of weapons and luxury goods, and the transfer of cash and other financial transactions.

UNDERSTANDING BETTER

MAKING A NUCLEAR THREAT

A video released in April 2013 by North Korea shows an imagined attack by the country against the United States. In the film, huge armed tanks move forwards, while synthesizer music plays in the background and a male voice delivers the message. The video shows the path North Korean missiles will take to hit Washington, DC, and other US cities, and fires explode on the map as the missiles hit the US targets. What do you think the North Korean government is trying to say with the release of this video? Do you think it is propaganda or a news story?

North Korea may be able to launch a nuclear missile in the future.

CHAPTER FIVE

Communism's future

North Korea remains the most Soviet-style communist country in the world. However, other communist countries have made small moves away from communism. China is one of those countries. Communism is also being debated in Vietnam.

THE FUTURE FOR CHINA

After many economic reforms that began in the 1970s, the economy in China is now labelled as a socialist market economy. There are still some state-owned industries, but many businesses are privately owned. It is very similar to a capitalist economy, and China has become the biggest exporter of goods in the world.

Despite the economic changes, Chinese citizens want the government to change as well. They want to know what their government is doing. This is because there is so much corruption among government officials, who can get away with this if the people are not aware of what they are doing. More and more Chinese citizens want the freedom to openly discuss political issues and receive information about their government's actions.

Shoppers crowd a busy street in China..

THE FUTURE FOR VIETNAM

In 2013, Vietnam's leaders asked for public comments on their plan to change the country's constitution. What happened instead was a public debate on the communist party's control of the government. The public discussed human rights, land ownership and wanting an army that was not tied to the communist party. People were warned not to speak against the party, so when journalist Nguyen Dac Kien criticized leaders, he was fired from his job at a state-run newspaper. Blogging is the only way to share information freely in Vietnam, but the government regularly puts bloggers in prison for expressing their views. According to the Reporters Without Borders organization, out of 180 countries only five have less media freedom than Vietnam.

Despite this lack of freedom, the economy is growing and the citizens of Vietnam are seeing their wages rise and healthcare and education improve. Like China, Vietnam is following a socialist market economy, but one where the state still controls most businesses.

UNDERSTANDING BETTER

POSTING POETRY ONLINE

Journalist Nguyen Dac Kien wrote a poem called "Freedom" that went viral once it was posted online. Here is an excerpt:

"If one day I have to go to prison, I'm certain it will be a communist prison, because I'm dying to be free."

What do you think this excerpt means? Why do you think Kien wrote this poem and put it online?

The lives of Vietnamese people are improving, but many are still unhappy with the communist government.

Cuba, Laos and North Korea

Economic troubles also affect the countries of Cuba, Laos and North Korea. Urgent solutions are needed there to be able to embrace the changing world markets.

CUBA

Cuba's economy has suffered, but it is also changing. In December 2012, the government authorized the creation of non-farming cooperatives, which allow people to set up small and medium-sized businesses. In 2015, after more than 50 years, the US and Cuba restored diplomatic relations. This could open up new trading opportunities and help the Cuban economy to grow.

LAOS

One of the poorest countries in eastern Asia, Laos depends on international donations to survive. Its economy, though, is growing fast, with a stock market opening in 2011 and big investment, particularly from China. Most of the new wealth, however, is concentrated in the towns and makes little difference to the rural poor.

Many children still live in poverty in Laos.

UNDERSTANDING BETTER

NORTH KOREAN REFUGEES

Every year, just a few thousand North Koreans manage to escape their tightly controlled country. Sokeel Park, who works for an organization called Liberty in North Korea (LiNK), interviews these refugees and helps them to start new lives in South Korea. Here is what Park said about how they escape from North Korea:

"Basically, people are dealing with either a frozen river, or trying to wade or swim across a river into China. And obviously, they have to deal with the border security on both sides – there's perhaps a couple of ways for people to deal with that. The main way is, actually, through corruption. And there are some people who just take the risk and try to make a run for it – but it's a really desperate measure to take."

What does this tell you about the people of North Korea? Why do you think they risk leaving the country when the dangers of doing so are so extreme?

NORTH KOREA

In North Korea, the future is uncertain for the country's government, whose leader, Kim Jong-un, is still fairly new. His father and grandfather had a strong cult of personality, but little is known about Kim Jong-un, who may not have as firm a hold over the government as his predecessors once did. The country continues to experience severe food shortages, while its people suffer the consequences.

North Korean soldiers patrol the country's border by boat.

What have you learnt?

Communism started becoming more popular around the world after the Industrial Revolution of the 1800s. As a large working class grew, class differences also grew. This working class provided the revolutionary force needed to overthrow the government of Russia, which became the first country under a communist system. Later, other countries staged revolutions and communist leaders took control. Communism reached its peak in the mid-1900s, but declined in the later part of the century. Only five countries now have communist political systems.

THE COMMUNIST SYSTEM

A communist system is a one-party political system, which means only the communist party can be in control of the government. Communist systems have been established through revolutions. Once in power, several communist leaders have also become dictators. A communist economy is a command economy, which means the government sets production goals for its country's industries. The industries produce goods to meet those goals and sell their goods at prices set by the government.

Mao Zedong's influence is still felt in China.

THE FUTURE

Economies are poor in most communist countries, except for China. Shortages often occur and citizens may not have enough food or goods for their families. They may turn to the black market and pay high prices for the food they need. With such tight controls, many citizens are speaking out for their rights. They want to freely use the internet and know what government officials are doing. They want the freedom to express their thoughts without fear of being imprisoned. And with the development of social media, information is reaching more people in a shorter time. It is not certain whether communism will survive far into the 2000s.

UNDERSTANDING BETTER

JUST AN ILLUSION?

British author Archie Brown wrote the following in his book *The Rise and Fall of Communism*:

"The idea of building communism, a society in which the state would have withered away, turned out to be a dangerous illusion."

What do you think the author means by this? Do you agree or disagree with his viewpoint?

A political poster in North Korea portrays an image of strength and wealth.

GLOSSARY

Bolshevik member of the Russian Social-Democratic Workers' party that seized control of the government in the 1917 Revolution

bourgeoisie wealthy, property-owning class in a country

capitalism economic system in which all land, houses and businesses belong to individuals, rather than the government

censorship to remove sections of a book, film or play, or block sites on the internet, which are thought to be harmful or a risk to the public

Cold War state of hostility that existed between the United States and the USSR, and their allies, between 1945 and 1990

collective group made up of a number of people to form new communities

command economy type of economy that is controlled by a central power and in which factories are publicly owned

communism system of government in which the state controls all wealth and property

constitution set of rules and principles that lays down how a nation should be governed

corruption dishonest actions by people in power

cult of personality extreme loyalty to a political leader, usually developed through the use of media and propaganda

dictator leader who rules with absolute power

elite group of people with privileges not available to everyone

human right something that all people should be allowed to have, regardless of who they are or where they live

intellectual person who is dedicated to learning and developing thoughts about certain subjects, such as politics or society

Iron Curtain political barrier that isolated an area of Europe under Soviet control during the Cold War

legislature branch of government that debates policy and makes laws

manifesto written statement declaring the views of its author

Marxism political and economic teachings of Karl Marx and Friedrich Engels

peasant person who works on a small farm

philosopher person who seeks wisdom through, study, thought and discussion

politburo group of people who oversee the communist party in China

proletariat urban working class in a country

propaganda spreading of information to influence public opinion or present a person in a favourable way

revolution violent upheaval to overthrow a ruler or bring about radical change

sanction law that prevents a country from buying goods from or selling them to other countries

socialist following the economic system in which land and industries are held by the government, rather than by people

tsar emperor of Russia

FIND OUT MORE

BOOKS

China (Journey Through), Liz Gogerly and Rob Hunt (Franklin Watts, 2016)

Marxism: A Graphic Guide (Introducing …), Rupert Woodfin and Oscar Zarate (Icon Books, 2009)

North Korea (Countries Around the World), Elizabeth Raum (Raintree, 2013)

The Cold War (Did Anything Good Come Out Of …), Paul Mason (Wayland, 2015)

WEBSITES

Learn more about communism at:
http://kids.britannica.com/elementary/article-352989/communism

Discover Russian history leading up to communist revolution at:
www.historyhome.co.uk/europe/russia1.htm

Find out more about Karl Marx at:
www.historylearningsite.co.uk/modern-world-history-1918-to-1980/russia-1900-to-1939/karl-marx/

See how communism works at:
www.howstuffworks.com/communism.htm

INDEX